THE UNWRITTEN RULES OF JOB SEARCHING

Learn How the Process Really Works,
and What You Need to Do

TIM LUCHTEFELD, MBA

Disclaimer notice

Compensation and taxes are discussed in this book. I am not a lawyer or accountant. This is based on personal experiences. For expert advice regarding those matters, please contact a tax or legal professional.

DEDICATION

This book is dedicated to my family: my father for being the best man I have ever known, my mother for her unending love and support, my sister for her pep talks, and of course, my beautiful and brilliant wife who has helped me every step of the way.

TABLE OF CONTENTS

PREFACE

When I decided to change my major from pre-med to business in college, I had no idea what I was doing. I knew I wanted a good job, but I had no idea what constituted a good job or where to even start. I felt like most of the advice online was hit or miss, and I had trouble distinguishing what was true from all the noise.

Thankfully, I have had tremendous mentors who have been influential in my journey. Much of their advice built the foundation of this book, and I tied in my personal experiences to round it out.

I wish a book like this would have existed for me in college. But so many of the books I tried to read seemed outdated or honestly full of fluff. I wanted a book full of pithy, actionable insights. And I hope I have provided just that.

INTRODUCTION

Let's be honest, searching for a job can be a grueling process. Especially if you are doing it for the first time out of college without a business background. You don't know what you don't know. It can be overwhelming.

Not to mention, everyone has their own opinion about it. Do this, not that, blah blah blah. From my experiences, it seems like a lot of job search advice comes from people who have not had to go through the process themselves for years.

There is no one right answer, but there are key things you can do to set yourself up for success. And I will share what I have done step by step to find job opportunities, land interviews, negotiate compensation, etc.

MY STORY

Let's rewind back to senior year. I am having the time of my life, but beyond graduation was that lurking challenge of getting a job and entering the "real world."

I had no idea how to land a job. My only experience was walking into the local grocery store in high school and asking for a job. It was way easier to not think about this next chapter of my life because it seemed so daunting.

Finally, I stopped procrastinating and asked a few adults how to find a job, and they told me to pick an industry and start applying on job boards... but I had no idea what an industry was! And I was clueless about job boards.

I had so many questions:

- How do I pick the right job?

- Where do I start?

- What is a fair salary?

- How do I pick a company that will not let me go in a year due to layoffs?

Through trial and error and seeking mentors, I was finally able to figure out how this job searching process works.

Eventually, I had three job offers on the table. And within a few years, I was making well into six figures and went back to earn my Master of Business Administration (MBA). After graduate school, I had several six-figure base salary job offers with annual bonuses and stock awards using this system.

All those opportunities came to fruition because of this system I created for myself, and I am going to walk you through it.

Please note the reason I am sharing this story with you is not to brag or because I think I am special. Rather I want to show that this is possible for you. Hopefully, you take this insight and go on to earn way more money than me! A rising tide lifts all boats.

Even if you don't know the first thing about business, I promise if you read this book in its entirety you will have the tools to effectively hit the ground running with your job search process.

Chapter 1

WHAT IS A BUSINESS?

We are starting at the beginning. I am going to assume you know absolutely nothing about the business world and this is the first time you have ever given it thought. (If you know about business, skip to Chapter 2). So, what is a business?

A business is a legal entity that provides value for customers in exchange for money. A famous quote about this phenomenon is "Price is what you pay; value is what you get."

Major businesses like Microsoft, Apple, Amazon, and McDonald's all do this. A hamburger costs a few dollars, the latest iPhone is over a thousand dollars, and Microsoft's solutions can cost a business millions of dollars.

For companies to deliver that value to customers, they hire employees. Employees need to deliver more value than they cost, otherwise the business may terminate that position.

Businesses range in size from small "mom and pop" shops to multinational Fortune 500 organizations. Companies operate in different industries. For example, Apple works in the technology industry, while McDonalds serves customers in the restaurant industry. These industries make up a country's economy.

At the end of the day, all businesses deliver value to customers through products or services, and in turn, they earn money.

GLOBAL ECONOMY

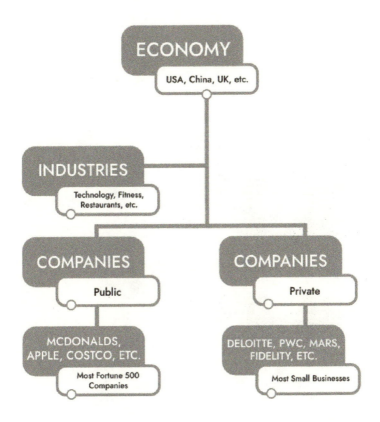

Chapter 2

WHAT COMPRISES A BUSINESS?

Businesses are made up of different functions. Most organizations have the following functions: finance, sales, marketing, technology, human resources, operations, and strategy. Within each function, there are several different departments as you can see on the graphic on the next page. Departments are made up of countless different positions.

It can get complicated and overwhelming with all the different types of positions and the various naming conventions for these positions. Not to mention, they are always changing the names of positions.

Some people have degrees that are prerequisites for their profession like accountants and engineers, while others do not have a formal university education that aligns with their current job. For example, companies like Microsoft, Google, Salesforce, or Amazon offer certifications that allow you to demonstrate technical knowledge in conjunction with your degree or in lieu of one.

Other professions, like sales, don't care what you studied in college. If you are a hard worker, proactive, open to learning, and a strong communicator, they will want to hire you. For reference, while working in sales for a leading healthcare technology company, people had majors in finance, information systems, biology, and history!

ORGANIZATIONAL STRUCTURE

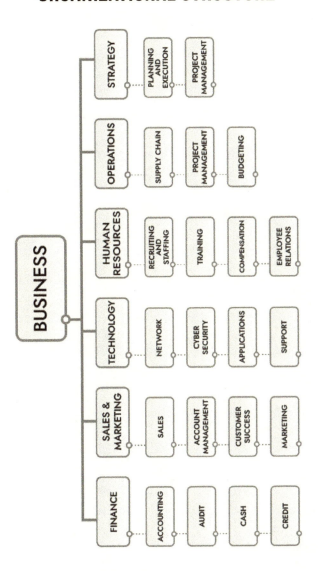

Note: This graphic is for educational purposes. Every company has their own unique organizational structure.

Chapter 3

WHERE DO YOU FIT IN?

An individual contributor role is the most common entry point for professionals entering the workforce for the first time. Individual contributor means you have a specific role but do not manage people. Business analysts, accountants, sales development representatives, recruiters, etc., are all examples of individual contributor roles.

Many high performing individual contributors will earn promotions and transition into management. Others want to avoid management and would prefer to grow as a skilled individual contributor.

An example is when you start in sales often you will be a business development representative making cold calls. For those of you who don't know, a cold call is when you call a potential customer out of the blue in hopes of selling your product or setting up a meeting in the future to potentially sell your product.

For easy math, let's say your goal is to set 100 meetings a year. And you set up 120. Since you exceeded expectations, you may be eligible for promotion to account executive. As an account executive you will receive new goals and if you are able to exceed them you can put yourself in a position to earn another promotion to become a senior account executive which comes with more money and responsibility.

Perhaps you really enjoyed the work as a business development representative, and you don't want to be an account executive. So, you work towards a management position over business development reps (BDR).

Don't get caught up in the titles, as they are always changing as the workforce evolves. Not to mention the same title for two different companies can be a completely different experience.

The key thing to understand is that if you want to manage people long-term, great! There is a career path for that. Or if you prefer to remain a skilled individual contributor, that is a viable option as well, but you will hit a professional ceiling at some point. But it's all about what works best for you in your situation.

MANAGEMENT STRUCTURE

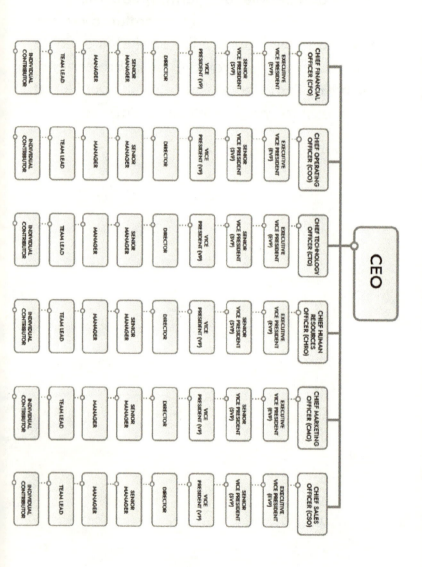

CAREER PATHS
Management vs. Individual Contributor

Chapter 4

LAYING THE FOUNDATION

No goal can be achieved without some sort of a plan. This book will give you a framework that has proven to be successful. You can use this framework to build your own plan that is specific to your unique situation. Everything I share with you is simple, but that doesn't mean it is easy to do.

What matters now is how you implement it. There is an expression: "Ideas are a dime a dozen; execution is all that matters." The more you invest in the process and prepare the better chance for success. It will take time and you may encounter tough obstacles but stick with it. And I know you can end up on the other side with a job offer in hand.

THE FRAMEWORK

VALUES

YOUR STORY

RESUME

LIST OF OPPORTUNITIES

REFERRALS

INTERVIEW PREPARATION

REVIEW JOB OFFERS

ACCEPT THE JOB!

Chapter 5

UNDERSTANDING YOUR VALUES

You need to identify your values. Values are what you consider to be of deep importance. Write out as many as you want but most people write out 5-10. Is money the most important thing in your life? Is it family? No judgment here from me.

This is your time to be honest with yourself to understand what is most important to you. Once you know what you value, it's easier to find the right profession or opportunity to strive towards. Otherwise, you might be stuck in a job that is not aligned with your values and you will want to quit.

When I did this exercise, this is how my values shook out.

VALUES	RANKING
Family	10
Stability	8
Money	7
Freedom	8
Work-Life Balance	9

For perspective, I am married with two dogs. My family is very important, which is why I ranked it a 10. I wanted a stable job, so I ranked it an 8. Now, nothing in life is guaranteed; I could lose my job tomorrow because of unforeseen circumstances, but when the company is pub-licly traded and has been around for a number of years, that risk is diminished relative to a startup. I ranked money a 7. I want to make enough money to provide for my family, but it's not the most important thing to me. I ranked freedom an 8. I wanted a role that would allow me to work remotely so I wouldn't have to make a morning commute and have more time in my day. Lastly, I ranked work-life balance a 9. I don't want to put in 80-hour weeks for my job just to get a bigger bonus. For me, that is not sustainable. But it is for other people. That is why it is so important to think about what it is you value, and how you see those values in a potential opportunity.

Don't be surprised if your values change over time. When I was single my values were very different. I wanted to travel the world and make as much money as I could, not caring about free time. Now that I am a bit older I view things differently.

Once you have your 5-10 values, rank them in importance and give them a score between 1-10. Keep these nearby, as they will be helpful when you are evaluating future job offers.

VALUES	RANKING

EXAMPLE VALUES

Achievement	Leadership
Advancement	Location
Challenging problems	Loyalty
Change	Meaningful work
Collaboration	Merit
Competition	Money
Cooperation	Personal development
Creativity	Physical challenge
Critical thinking	Pleasure
Decisiveness	Power and authority
Effectiveness	Privacy
Environment	Promotion
Ethical practice	Public service
Excellence	Quality

Family

Fast pace

Financial gain

Flexibility

Freedom

Friendships

Growth

Having a family

Helping others/society

Honesty

Inclusion

Independence

Influencing others

Recognition

Religion

Reputation

Responsibility

Security

Self-respect

Sophistication

Stability

Status

Supervising others

Teamwork

Wealth

Work-life balance

Chapter 6

TELLING YOUR STORY

Interviewing is all about being able to tell your story. We all have a story to tell. You are unique in your own way, and it is your job as a candidate to be able to tell your story to the interviewer.

Think about it. Stories move us. They are all around us from the movies we watch, the shows we binge on Netflix, or the funny encounters we have day to day that we share with loved ones.

When you are getting ready to go into an interview, think about your story and what you bring to the table. Don't just focus on the facts and statistics.

Recruiters and hiring managers want to know not only that you are qualified for the position but why you want the job. They want to make sure you are a good fit and will not quit in six months. Put yourself in their shoes. Would they want to hire someone only motivated by the money? Or someone who seems passionate about the work? I can assure you they will prefer the latter.

We will cover interview questions to prepare for in Chapter 14, and this will help you lay a foundation for a successful story.

TELLING YOUR STORY

	YOU WITH YOUR STORY	OTHER CANDIDATE
JOB SKILLS	✓	✓
EFFECTIVE COMMUNICATOR	✓	✗
ABILITY TO INFLUENCE	✓	✗
PREPARATION	✓	✗

Chapter 7

CRAFTING THE PERFECT RESUME

Almost every single employer will require a resume. An important thing to know about resumes is that everyone has their own opinion about them. There is not one right way to do them, but there are wrong ways to do them.

Keep in mind that your resume should be telling your story and not just listing random accomplishments. Every word on your resume should be carefully considered. Each bullet point needs to set you up to tell a great little story.

FORMAT

People will argue all day over which format is best for a resume. Or someone may try to sell you a resume format that is guaranteed to work for only $999. In my opinion, these people are charlatans, or at best, working with executives. There is no silver bullet with one format, but some styles do work better than others. For example, if you are applying for a role that is in graphic design or is more creative, a colorful resume may resonate better than a traditional black and white resume.

Conversely, if you are applying for a consulting role or in the banking industry, a standard resume makes sense. There are some timeless, classic resume formats like Chicago Booth resume which you can easily find online.

LENGTH

Your resume doesn't need to be longer than a page. Keep it simple.

PICTURE

I would not put my picture on the resume. That is what LinkedIn is for these days.

DOS

- Each bullet point is an achievement or something you can elaborate on if questioned

- Strong, pithy language

- Tailored to the opportunity

- Quantified and specific

DON'TS

- Grammatical errors, misspellings

- Listing job responsibilities and not achievements

- Being general and vague

- Focusing on "we" instead of "I"

Let's go over a quick example. Pretend this is a bullet point on a marketing resume: "Worked on a successful marketing campaign" vs. "Created a video marketing campaign that generated over $70,000 in revenue for the company."

The second example is better because it is not only descriptive, but it clearly articulates your contributions and the direct impact on the business. The first example is vague and generic, and it is not really communicating much value to the interviewer. They have no way of knowing your role in the marketing campaign and the outcome of it.

Lastly, when it comes to resumes, it is best to tailor each resume to the unique opportunity to which you are applying. This is best practice and will separate you from the other pool of candidates.

RESUME VERBS

LEADERSHIP VERBS	IMPROVEMENT VERBS	ADDITIONAL VERBS
Appointed	Accelerated	Accomplished
Challenged	Amended	Activated
Conducted	Amplified	Acquired
Controlled	Augmented	Advertised
Coordinated	Arranged	Analyzed
Developed	Balanced	Assess
Distributed	Broaden	Arranged
Enforced	Centralized	Attainted
Executed	Clarified	Compiled
Governed	Consolidate	Created
Guided	Decreased	Cultivated
Handled	Enhanced	Designed
Hired	Formalized	Discovered

Initiated	Fortified	Documented
Instructed	Improved	Drafted
Interviewed	Increased	Established
Managed	Innovated	Estimated
Monitored	Minimized	Fulfilled
Motivated	Modified	Guided
Presided	Optimized	Handled
Regulated	Overhauled	Launched
Scheduled	Redesigned	Maintained
Staged	Refined	Obtained
Stimulated	Reorganized	Presented
Strategized	Replaced	Procured
Supervised	Resolved	Reported
Trained	Revamped	Solved
Tutored	Simplified	Streamlined

Chapter 8

YOUR BRAND

The expression "your brand" is grossly over-used and misused. Your brand does not mean you need to post incessantly on various social media platforms about how great you are.

Rather, I think Jeff Bezos said it best: "Your brand is what people say about you when you are not in the room."

People have all types of brands because personalities are all over the spectrum: loud, quiet, introverted, extroverted, analytical, emotional, open, reserved, etc. You get the picture. Now, it is true you can find a job with just a resume and no online presence. However, it helps if you do have an online presence. And perhaps you are someone like me, who cringes at the thought of having my face plastered all over the internet. Well, rest assured, there is a happy medium.

One tool you will want to set up is a LinkedIn account. People have described it as the Facebook of business. It allows you to connect with other people, but most of the content is focused on business.

Most recruiters want to see your LinkedIn when applying for jobs. Think of your profile as a public resume. It's a quick way to verify that you are a real person and see if there are any mutual connections.

I strongly recommend you setting up a LinkedIn profile if you don't have one yet. Microsoft owns it, and don't anticipate it going away anytime soon.

Chapter 9

FINDING OPPORTUNITIES

Finding the right opportunity is not an easy task. It is even more challenging when you have no idea what you want to do. If you find yourself in that position, do not fret. But you are going to have to draw some lines in the sand at some point. Otherwise, you will stay stationary and make no progress at all. Better to try something and learn then to do nothing at all.

There are a litany of tools and online job boards that you can use to help find opportunities, a few of them include LinkedIn, Indeed, ZipRecruiter, and Handshake.

Most people will spend time perusing all the openings and applying for anything they feel is a good fit. This can turn into a big waste of time if you are not careful. Too many people will start applying to as many jobs as they can and only focusing on quantity over quality.

And perhaps you could even stumble into a couple interviews, but it may not be with firms you want to work for. More likely you will end up wasting hours applying for jobs that don't even align with your values.

Example if you highly value family and don't want to travel for work then why waste your time applying for roles that require you to travel once a week? Or perhaps you want a remote only role, but you are applying for jobs that require you to be in office. This runs counterintuitive to what you want. You may think, *Well, I might be able to negotiate some remote work.* Perhaps you will be able to but that is a lot of extra work just a possibility rather than a certainty.

From my experience, a better way to leverage these tools is to create automated alerts for very specific criteria for you. For example, let's say you want to get a job in marketing, and you are fresh out of college. You should consider creating an email alert for "Marketing Specialist" opportunities with a defined geography. Perhaps you want to work remote, or you are open to relocation you should adjust your parameters accordingly.

Now in your inbox you will have several marketing specialist opportunities, and you can comb through them to see which ones you even want to apply for instead of just googling jobs in marketing, going down a rabbit hole and ending up on YouTube or TikTok watching another mindless video (speaking from personal experience)!

However, when you find the right opportunity, hold off on applying. We are going to talk about how to increase your chances of making it to the first-round interview in the next few chapters.

FINDING OPPORTUNITIES

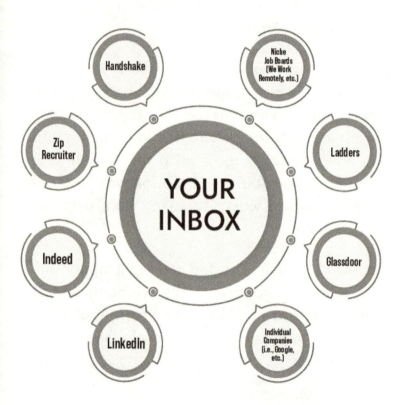

Chapter 10

INTERVIEW STRUCTURE

Every company is different with how they interview, but usually the process involves anywhere from 3-6 rounds of interviews involving the recruiter, the hiring manager, peers, cross functional teams, or other professionals.

Most of the time the first round will be a 30-minute phone call with a recruiter. They will ask you questions like:

- Tell me about yourself.

- What are your salary expectations?

- Why this company?

- Why this role?

- Are you interviewing anywhere else?

Don't worry, we will go over how to answer these questions in Chapter 14.

If you make it past the first round, the next interview is often with the hiring manager.

The hiring manager is the person who will be your boss if you get the job. Therefore, it's important to try to see if you can picture yourself working for this individual if offered the job.

Granted, that is a difficult feat because you have such a short time window, and it is hard to know what they are like day to day. But at least keep your eyes open for any jarring red flags.

If you make it past the hiring manager, then likely they will want to see how you connect with a peer or someone you may need to work closely with on a frequent basis.

Sometimes organizations will throw in additional rounds from people with various perspectives.

The last round is usually reserved for someone who is higher in the organization or a panel interview where there are several people.

Depending on the type of role, they may have a final assessment for you at this time. Assessments will vary depending on the type of role you are pursuing. Below are a few examples of assessments, but this list is not all encompassing.

SALES—ROLE PLAY OR PRESENTATION

For most sales roles you will do some type of role play or presentation. If a role play, oftentimes the interviewer will provide you a fictional scenario to prepare for ahead of time. They want to see how you communicate, how you prepare, how you handle objections in the moment. In essence their thought process is if you can handle a role play or presentation then you will be able to succeed in the role.

CUSTOMER SUCCESS MANAGER—PRODUCT DEMO OR PRESENTATION

Similar to sales you may have to give a presentation, or they will give you access to their software to review and see how you handle a product demo. In addition to evaluating your communication skills, they want to see if you are able to learn new things quickly.

CONSULTANT—CASE STUDY

A case study is a staple for consulting interviews. If you are unfamiliar with case studies, these are scenarios that try to simulate aspects of consulting projects that you must solve on the spot. The interviewer is trying to see how you think, what questions you ask, how you communicate, are you quick on your feet. There is not always one right answer for case studies. These case studies can vary widely. If you are interested in learning more, just do a Google search for how best to prepare for a case study at BCG, McKinsey or Bain (three of the most prestigious consulting firms) and you will find countless resources and programs to help you prepare.

- Sales / Account Executive – Role play or presentation

- Customer Success Manager – Product demo

- Consultant – Case study

INTERVIEW PROCESS

Application Submitted (200 Applicants)

Resume Scan (100 Applicants)

Keyword Scan (50 Applicants)

First Round Interview — Recruiter (10 Applicants)

Second Round Interview — Hiring Manager (6 Applicants)

Third Round (4 Applicants)

Final Round (2 Applicants)

Offer (1 Applicant)

Chapter 11

THE APPLICANT TRACKING SYSTEM (ATS)

Companies use a tool called the applicant tracking system (ATS) to help their recruiting efforts. Think of it as a big funnel (image on next page). This allows them to keep all the candidates stored in one place and quickly filter through all the applications.

The company will set up the system to look for specific words related to their function. For example, keywords for marketing roles may include: "campaign, segmentation, ROI, branding, promotions, customer journey", etc. If you submit a resume that has none of these keywords, it will be discarded, and you will be disqualified for the job.

You won't ever know for certain what keywords are searching for in their applicants. So instead of trying to game the system we are going to discuss a more effective way to circumvent the ATS in the next chapter.

BIG COMPANIES VS. SMALL COMPANIES

Larger organizations tend to rely more on the ATS systems because of the volume of applications they have to process. For example, think about Google. According to an article published by CNBC, "Year after year, Google has been ranked as one of the top companies to work for, so it's no surprise that the tech giant receives roughly three million applications per year. With an acceptance rate of 0.2%, you'd have a better chance of getting into Harvard" (Popomaronis, 2019).

Compared to a regional company that has only a few hundred employees, they may not need as many automated systems to process applications quickly.

Do not be surprised if it takes longer with larger employers with more screenings. That is very common given their size and internal rules for hiring. The interview process can take 4-6 weeks if not longer sometimes.

Smaller companies can often move more swiftly and can have a less structured approach. Because of their nimble size they can complete the entire process as fast as 1-3 weeks. One process isn't necessarily better than the other, but it is good to note to properly manage expectations.

APPLICANT TRACKING SYSTEM (ATS)

First Round Interview

Chapter 12

EXECUTING THE REFERRAL

One of the best ways to land a first-round interview is to know someone at the company and have them refer you for a role. The higher up in the organization that person is, the more influential that referral is going to be for you. For example, I was fortunate enough to have a referral at Boston Consulting Group (BCG is a premiere consulting firm that frequently hires from the Ivy League schools), and I made it to the final round, but I blew the interview. The people I was competing against were from the top schools in the country, and my background was in a decent state school, to put it nicely.

But the point I am driving home here is that referrals can help level the playing field. It can open doors that were previously closed. But you might be thinking, *Well, you had connections at BCG. I don't have those connections.* You are right; by dumb luck I did have one connection. But people I have helped have landed jobs at various Fortune 500 companies and startups without having family or friends at these companies. I will tell you how, but let's cover some background first.

WHAT IS THE SIGNIFICANCE OF A REFERRAL?

A referral is so helpful because it allows you to circumvent the Applicant Tracking System (ATS) that we discussed earlier. Most of the time it immediately puts you on a short list for being considered for a first-round interview. Granted if you have no relevant experience that is needed for the role, then most likely they will not grant you an interview. But if you are in earshot of the requirements and have a solid resume, then there is a high likelihood you will land a first-round interview.

One conversation I had with a recruiter at a prominent Fortune 500 company told me that they hire 35% of new employees from referrals. At this organization, if an individual receives a referral, it is valid for one year. Meaning even if the opportunity they are targeting does not work out, they are automatically put on a short list of considered candidates for any future opportunities for the rest of that one-year period. Now, not every company operates like that, but most companies want their employees to refer talent.

WHO TO REACH OUT TO FOR A REFERRAL

Alright, so you may be wondering how to get this referral. Start by scanning your network including but not limited to alumni, friends, family, past acquaintances and even strangers. Avoid recruiters! This may sound counterintuitive, but recruiters are inundated with messages. Chances are they won't even take the time to read your note. You want to reach out to someone who doesn't get a lot of messages so that they are more likely to respond to you.

When reaching out, try to target someone who is in the current role you want or a position or two above you. Do not go for the top executives and do not go for people below you. The executives will be most likely too busy to respond to your messages (unless it's a small company, then there can be exceptions). And people below you in the organization may not want to refer you for a role that is above them. They would see you as competition. Therefore, targeting someone in the role you want or, even better, right above you will be more likely to chat with you. Especially, someone that is a level above the role you want because they are less likely to see you as a threat and will have more influence in the open position you are pursuing.

HOW DOES THIS ACTUALLY WORK?

For example, let's say you want to work as an account executive at a company like Stryker. And you have no connections there through family, friends, alumni etc. You can go on LinkedIn (which we discussed in Chapter 8) and find countless strangers who work as account executives at Stryker and send them a message.

I have seen tremendous success with a simple message written like the one below.

Hi ____,

I know this message is out of the blue. I'm a student at _____ looking at the account executive opportunity at Stryker.

Would you be open to chatting for a few minutes about your experiences there? If not, all is well.

Best,

____

(xxx) xxx - xxxx

Why does this message work?

This message works for several reasons:

- acknowledges the message is from a stranger

- clearly states why you are reaching out

- tailored for that person and organization

- gives them a chance to decline with no hard feelings

- people remember what it is like to be a student and want to help other students

(**Side note**: This works even if you are not a student, but can be more effective to play the student card.)

Now, not everyone will respond or be open to chatting with you, but some people will be willing to help.

Once someone agrees to chat with you, then you need to make sure you prepare to the best of your ability. You need to have a general understanding of the company, their role, and the long-term vision of the company so that you can demonstrate you have done your homework and are asking strategic questions. Most of that information is on the company website, so it shouldn't be too challenging to find and read.

When you have that 15-30 minute conversation with that individual, this should be your
rough structure:

1. Greetings & thank them

2. Proposed agenda

3. Background

4. Questions

5. Referral

6. Closing & thank them

GREETINGS / THANK THEM

Exchange pleasantries. Then always follow with
a thank you. This person is taking time out of
their day to do you a favor. Common courtesy
is to show gratitude by thanking them.

PROPOSED AGENDA

After that, propose a brief agenda. This doesn't
have to be formal but rather gives the person
on the call a better idea of what you are trying

to get out of it. For example, you can say something like:

> "Hi, ___. Thanks again for taking the time to chat with me today. As I mentioned in my first note, I am interested in _____. If it is alright with you, I'd like to give you a brief background about myself, learn more about _____ from your perspective, and ask you a few questions about your experiences with the organization. How does that sound?

Invariably, they will say yes and will appreciate there being more structure to the call so they can have an idea of what is coming next.

GIVE BACKGROUND

Provide a brief background of your professional experience and keep it high level. Keep it under a minute or two, as you don't want to waste half the call talking about yourself.

ASK STRATEGIC QUESTIONS

This is where you can really learn about the role and company. A few questions you can ask include:

- How is success measured in the role?

- What separates a great performer from a good performer?

- What are your thoughts on the company culture?

Stay away from asking about how much money they make. People can get weird about money, and you don't want to make them feel uncomfortable.

ASKING FOR THE REFERRAL

Now, if the conversation is going well, you don't want to end the conversation without asking for a referral. Some people are kind enough to offer it without you having to ask, but chances are you will have to ask. A few different ways of how you can ask are below, depending on your communication style.

"I have really enjoyed our conversation and would love to work at _____. What advice would you have for me to earn an opportunity there?"

"Given the competitive job market and this great opportunity would you be open to referring me for this role? If you don't feel comfortable, I completely understand."

"Based on our conversation, my background, and experience, do you think I could potentially be a fit for this role? If so, would you be open to referring to help my chances in landing a first-round interview?"

There are countless ways to ask this question. Do what feels best for you. Some people might say no, and that is alright. I would thank them for their time and ask if it would be acceptable for you to follow up with them in the future if you have additional questions about the role or company. You want to make sure you are leaving the door open.

But if they say yes, then you are in great shape. You need to ask them about next steps. Clarify if they need to fill out something internally or if you merely need to list their name on the application. Most of the time people won't know off the top of their heads and will need to look into it for you.

Hold off on applying until you get a definitive answer from them. Because if they need to submit something internally then often you will get a special link to apply for the job instead of the one posted publicly for everyone. But if they tell you to just apply online and enter their email and name, that works, too. One is not better than the other. Every organization is different.

WHY WOULD SOMEONE REFER YOU?

Most people who have been successful are kind and want to help other people succeed. Now, of course there are bad apples in this world, but most people are not like that. If you are honest, genuine, and curious you will be amazed how many people are willing to help you.

In addition, many companies offer a referral bonus (~$500–$2,500, depending on position and the organization) for their employees. However, to receive the bonus, the referred individual needs to be hired and work for the organization for a specified amount of time, usually somewhere between 6 months to a year.

HOW IT WORKS

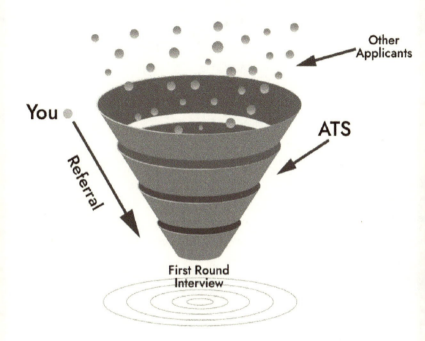

Other Applicants

You

ATS

Referral

First Round Interview

Chapter 13

PREPARATION—RESEARCHING THE COMPANY

Preparing for your first-round interview is crucial. This can help separate you from all the other candidates. Many people do the bare minimum in preparing for an interview and some, foolishly, do nothing at all.

But if you do quite a bit of due diligence, it can help you stick out during the interview process.

HOW TO PREPARE

Build off the foundation of knowledge you started to acquire when preparing and speaking with the individual who referred you for the current role. You want to understand and be able to articulate several different aspects:

- brief overview of the company history

- the business model (aka how they make money)

- the strategic vision for the company

- any recent articles in the news about the company

- some companies will even have blog posts about the specific role you are interviewing for

- biggest competitors

- culture—Glassdoor, employees

- overview of the market structure

Most of this information will be available on the company's website or YouTube channel. Often if it's a public company, there will be more information available then if it is a private company due to different legal requirements.

PUBLIC COMPANIES

ANNUAL REPORT (10-K)

Pull up the company's website and visit the investor relations part of the website. Here you will find a wealth of information about the business. Every year a company will file something called 10-k. This is a document required for the United States Securities and Exchange Commission (SEC). It's a comprehensive report that will have detailed financials and often will articulate the strategy of the business. It can be a great resource to provide a holistic view of the company. Don't worry about trying to understand everything in the filing. This is meant to help build up your general knowledge.

QUARTERLY REPORT (10-Q)

Every fiscal quarter (3 months), a public company will present their results. These reports are less in depth as the annual 10-k filing but can give a great pulse check on how the company is currently doing.

EARNINGS CALL

The executive leadership team (CEO, CFO, and other executives) will have an earnings call discussing the results in the quarterly report. These calls are recorded and publicly posted. You can listen to them to better understand the business. Most of the time, the beginning of the call discusses the financials in depth and can be less important for you compared to the middle and towards the end of the call when the executive team will answer questions from investors. This can be a great glimpse into how the executives think about the company.

PRIVATE COMPANIES

It can be hit or miss trying to find information on private companies. Some put a ton of great information online for you to devour while others can seem like a black box and hard to understand. When that is the case, just do your best to learn as much as you can.

Check out their website, YouTube channel, press releases, etc. Any little nugget can help when interviewing.

If you can't find any information online, don't hesitate to reach out to someone that works at the company to pick their brain as discussed in Chapter 12. It can be a great opportunity to learn a completely different perspective. You can potentially use that insight to answer questions later during the interview. This demonstrates to the interviewer you are really doing your homework before the interview. We will cover a specific example in Chapter 14 about answering the question: Why do you want to work here?

CULTURE

Company culture can be a difficult thing to quantify and understand. It means different things to different people. Every company says they have an amazing culture. In reality, some do, and others don't.

Thankfully, tools like Glassdoor exist. It is an anonymized platform where people will rate their employers and share their experiences.

While Glassdoor is a powerful resource, some companies will make employees sign agreements saying they won't disparage their employer on any online forum, and if they do, the company has the right to pursue litigation. If a company seems "too good to be true" it probably is.

But you can go on LinkedIn and search for people that have worked there in the past. If you see a bunch of people lasting only 6 months or 1 year, it may be a sign of a problematic company culture. You can even reach out to these people to get another perspective. But keep in mind that is also one person's perspective.

THE INTERVIEWER

If you really want to go the extra mile in prepping for your interview, then do a google search of the person you will be speaking with for the interview. See if they are a subject matter expert in their domain and have published any blogs, podcasts, books etc. If you can find any of this content and you can review it and formulate thoughtful questions in the interview, this will separate you from the majority of candidates. We will go over an example in a bit.

WHY PREPARE SO MUCH?

When you take the time to prepare and learn the nuances of the business, the recruiter or hiring manager will appreciate the fact that you took the time to learn about the company. It shows initiative, and that you are proactive and invested in this process and the company. Some hiring managers even look at a candidate's willingness to prepare as an indicator of how hard they may work if offered an opportunity. Not to mention, the more you prepare the more confident you will feel. That confidence will radiate from you and further increase your chances of making it to the next round or getting that elusive offer.

PILLARS OF PREPARATION

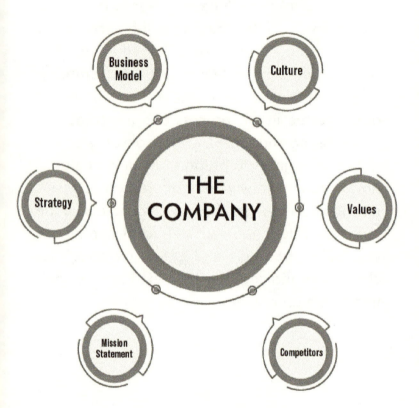

Chapter 14

PREPARATION—INTERVIEW QUESTIONS

After you have a solid foundation of the company, you need to work on preparing for questions they will ask. Now, we don't have a crystal ball to know what exactly they are going to ask, but one, a couple, or many of the questions listed below may be asked.

THE ESSENTIALS

TELL ME ABOUT YOURSELF

This is an easy icebreaker for the recruiter to ask. It gives them a chance to learn about you, and it provides you the opportunity to showcase your storytelling abilities. Have a concise and pithy story to share. There isn't one right way to do this, but many wrong ways, such as rambling about experiences that are not pertinent to the discussion, focusing only on personal stories, or not having anything to share.

At the end of your story, the interviewer may ask a specific question about your experiences, or it can be a natural time to ask why you are looking for a job, so be ready for that.

Here was my example:

> "I double majored in management information systems and marketing. Upon graduation, I started working for Omnicell as an implementation consultant traveling the country. If you are not familiar with Omnicell, they are the leading healthcare technology company that offers medication management solutions and enterprise software. My role was to optimize those solutions and work with directors of pharmacy to optimize workflow from the pharmacy to the operating room. After a year, I earned an opportunity to relocate to Pittsburgh, PA, for a

sales role. Here I sold multimillion dollar contracts to the C-suite of the largest hospitals in the Midwest. It required critical communication skills and persistence to get through those arduous contraction negotiations. Realizing I wanted to make a change and move into strategy long term, I went back to school to earn my MBA. I am finishing up grad school here in May and that's why I am excited to be speaking to you today as a potential next chapter."

Note: Sometimes people say you need to have it be a 60-second elevator pitch, while others say you should go longer. There is not one right way. Do what works best for you, and clearly tell a story that the interviewer can follow. It's more important to be remembered than to adhere to a strict 60-second policy.

Also, notice how my example ends with an easy segue to answer why I want to work at the company. In a way, I am trying to steer the conversation in a way for me to show I have done my homework and set them up to ask an organic next question.

POTENTIAL STUDENT ELEVATOR PITCH

> "I majored in history and finished with a 3.5 GPA. But after graduation I had trouble finding an opportunity to directly use my degree. So, I made the decisions to pivot and focus my efforts on putting myself in a position to earn a sales opportunity. I have been reading sales books like *The Challenger Sale* and reaching out to people in my network who work in sales to learn more about the profession and best practices. That is why I am so excited to be having a conversation here with you about this sales opportunity."

This is a generic example I came up with for the book for educational purposes, but you can see how this would be effective. It communicates how you ended up here today exploring this conversation and what you are doing to make this transition from historian to sales professional. Most people value authenticity and will appreciate the honesty. If anything, you can use this to set yourself apart by showing how you are willing to pivot when necessary and will work hard to educate yourself to put yourself in a position to succeed.

WHY US?

Recruiters love to ask why you are interested in their company. You should have a good answer ready to go on command. Make sure to say something that is unique to that company. If you give an answer that is so vague it can apply to hundreds of other companies, then they won't think you are invested in them.

Example

"I'd love to work at _____ for two main reasons. The first is they are the market leader in _____, and they have helped customers like _____ achieve better results by _____.

Second is because of culture. I have read the Glassdoor reviews and they are overwhelmingly positive. In addition, I had a chance to connect with [insert person you spoke with] _____ prior to this interview, and they told me their favorite thing about the company is _____, which just contributes to the phenomenal culture at _____."

Notice in this example it subtly weaves in the preparation work you have done for this interview by pointing out you researched them on

Glassdoor and had conversations with personnel at the organization. This subtly shows the interviewer that you did your homework without having to come out and tell them, "I prepared a lot for this interview."

WHY THIS POSITION?

The recruiter or hiring manager wants to know why you want to work in this specific position. They want to see if you understand what the day-to-day type of work will be. They want to ensure you don't hate it three months into the job and want to quit. Like previous questions, there are a myriad of correct answers if they are genuine and specific. You can't say something like, "I want this job because it pays a lot." Even if that is the truth for you then you need to learn how to craft your answer to be a bit more diplomatic.

Example

Why Sales?

"That's a great question. I would say there are two main reasons. The first is that sales is a dynamic environment where you get to help customers solve unique challenges and I find that very rewarding. Secondly, working in sales gives you the unique opportunity where your compensation is often directly aligned with your performance and how hard you work. The harder you work the better your performance will be and subsequently the rewards."

WHAT IS YOUR GREATEST WEAKNESS?

These can be trickier questions. You can't say, "I don't know", "I don't have any", or "I work too hard." People will roll their eyes, and it's a sign of lacking self-awareness. You do want to say a weakness and be genuine about it. But at the same time make sure the weakness you are saying is not the core requirement for the role you are interviewing for, and you inadvertently disqualify yourself.

Meaning, if you are interviewing for a data scientist role don't say your greatest weakness is working with complex data sets. Focus on a different area that is important but not at the crux of your job. Like you could say you want to work on communication and have an example ready to share. The key to answering this question is to be self-aware enough that your weakness is genuine, you know it's a weakness, and what you are doing to improve it.

Example

"I would say the greatest opportunity for me to improve is in verbal communication. I tend to be a very analytical individual who prefers to communicate in written formats; however, I understand the importance of being able to communicate verbally with diverse stakeholders. To work on this skill, I have been reading several different communication books such as ____, ____, and ____ to help me improve."

WHAT IS YOUR PROUDEST ACHIEVEMENT?

People like to ask this question because it gives a glimpse into what you value. It helps the people interviewing you understand what drives you. It's nice if your answer can tie back into the role or with the company so the interview can draw parallels from your experience and see how they are applicable to the role you are interviewing for. But if you can't, it is alright. Just do your best to articulate clearly the "why" behind your proudest accomplishment.

Example (Student)

"My proudest accomplishment was when I was elected president of the student council because it showed me how much my peers trust me to help move us forward. And for me to earn that position, I had to create a plan and implement it effectively to earn that special opportunity. I am proud that I was able to do that effectively."

WHAT'S YOUR DESIRED SALARY?

Don't answer it. People want to tie you to this number to get you to work for cheaper. Also, don't share past compensation unless it is to raise your current earning potential.

This question is very common for recruiters to ask. Before you outright just give a number, I would encourage you to answer the question with a question.

"That's a fair question, could you help me understand all the components of the compensation package and the ranges you are offering for this role?"

Don't be surprised if when discussing compensation if there are more pauses and silence then the prior conversation. That is completely normal. You will learn to embrace the silence.

There is a lot more than just salary when it comes to compensation packages. Salary is a big component but not the only one. There can be commission, bonuses, 401ks (retirement plans), employee stock purchase plans (ESPP), restricted stock units (RSUs), paid time off (PTO), benefits, etc. We will cover this in more detail in Chapter 18.

When it comes to salary, most of the time companies have different ranges they are pursuing for roles. If the recruiter tells you the role ranges from 45k-70k starting salary depending on experience, then at least now you have an idea what to expect and what may be reasonable to negotiate.

Now, if the recruiter won't share any ranges when it comes to compensation, I would urge you to stay strong and deflect if possible. You can say something like

"I don't really feel comfortable sharing a salary number without understanding other parts of the compensation package. Perhaps, if you can share any insight about what people in this role typically earn, we can see if we are aligned."

Keep in mind, most of the time the recruiters will be transparent with you about the range of earnings. If they aren't, then that is indicative of the type of organization they are. And you can ask yourself if they are not transparent about this, what else are they not being transparent about? Just something to think about as you go through this process.

After answering those essential questions, they may start to ask you behavioral-based questions or they could wait until the next round to ask them.

ADDITIONAL QUESTIONS TO BE THINKING ABOUT

- How would your peers describe you in one word?

- What's been the best working relationship with a boss and why?

- Can you describe what this role is?

- Where do you see yourself in five years?

- Why do you want this job?

- How did you learn about this job?

BEHAVIORAL-BASED QUESTIONS

These types of questions are scenario-based questions. They are trying to understand more about you at a deeper level. When answering these questions, you really want to be focused on you and saying "I" instead of "we", because they are looking at hiring you, not your old team. The company wants to know three key things about you.

- Do they like you?

- Can you do the job?

- Will you get along with the team?

There is a specific format to answer these questions successfully. It is called the STAR format. It's a framework that helps you communicate a story in a concise format

- S – **Situation**: What was the situation?

- T – **Task**: What was the task at hand?

- A – **Action**: What was the action you took to accomplish the task in this situation?

- R – **Result**: What was the result because of the action you took to accomplish the task?

Like the questions listed in the essentials above, we don't know every question, but there are common ones.

CAN YOU TELL ME ABOUT A TIME YOU HAD TO CHANGE SOMEONE'S OPINION?

No matter what job you land, you will need to have the ability to change someone's opinion. Whether you are in customer service and have an angry customer. Or you are in sales trying to persuade a new prospect to be a client. Perhaps you may have to get your manager's buy in for a new project, the ability to influence is critical. Companies know this and that's why they want to hear about a time you were able to be persuasive.

"There was this one time during my internship when we had a very upset customer because their product wasn't working properly. I took the time to listen to the customer and realized it wasn't only the fact that the product wasn't working that was leading to the frustration, but the lack of communication for them. By taking the time to listen first, I was able to find someone to help them internally to resolve the problem.

Additionally, I assured them that the lack of communication they experienced was due to a few bugs in the new system we just went live with and will not happen again.. The customer was thankful that I took the time to listen and went out of my way to explain why the miscommunication occurred in the first place. By the end of the call, he was in a good mood and gave a 5/5 on service today."

Let's break it down, using the STAR formula:

Situation – There is an angry customer.

Task – Solve their problem and make the customer less angry.

Action – Listened to the customer to understand the root cause of the issue. Reached out to someone internally to resolve the issue. Communicated back to the client how this will not be an issue going forward.

Results – The customer's problem was solved, and we got 5/5 stars.

TELL ME ABOUT A TIME YOU HAD TO HANDLE CONFLICT

Conflict is everywhere in the workplace. We are human beings and there will be times when you disagree with peers, management, clients, etc. Employers want to know how you handle conflict and overcome it. Do you let it consume you? Do you have a "win at all costs" personality that will be a detriment to team performance and cohesion? Or are you able to navigate those challenging situations and ultimately achieve the goal at hand?

When answering this question do NOT put the blame at the other person. They don't want to hear about how awful a former coworker, classmate, peer was to you. In addition, when giving an example story be sure to avoid saying you had any conflicts about politics, religion, etc. Those topics can be emotionally charged and make people feel uncomfortable. Generally, it is best to avoid them in the workplace.

There was one time after the company went through a large restructuring, the pricing team had to relocate from sunny California to rainy Pittsburgh, Pennsylvania. There was one individual on the pricing team who became my new point of contact. She would help me get contracts out the door for clients, and we had been experiencing a massive increase in contract requests with growing wait times. This led to friction among us and the team. Instead of ignoring and plowing forward, I set up a time to learn what was bothering her, what was on her plate, and how we can work more effectively. I learned the transition for her had been especially tough, and in addition. She preferred to communicate through email when a high priority item needed to be discussed. Traditionally, I preferred to converse over the phone. We came up with our own system to prioritize different items via email with specific subject headlines for high priority items. This new system helped us reduce turnaround time by 2-3

days per contract and our working relationship drastically improved. Because sometimes
it goes back to the little things of just knowing
how people prefer to communicate.

Star – There was friction between me and a
coworker.

Task – We had to find a way to reduce contract
turnaround time and improve our working relationship.

Action – I set up time to listen and craft a careful plan.

Result – We were able to streamline the con-
tracting process and reduce turnaround time
by 2-3 days while improving our communication with one another.

TELL ME ABOUT A TIME YOU HAD TO MAKE A DECISION WHEN YOU DIDN'T HAVE ALL OF THE INFORMATION

Employers want to see how you think. They
want to know you are an independent thinker.
Providing a crisp answer illustrates your abili-

ty to operate without constant supervision and don't suffer from "analysis paralysis."

TELL ME ABOUT A TIME YOU HAD TO BE VERY PERSISTENT TO HIT YOUR GOALS, AND HOW YOU DID IT

Work is a marathon, not a sprint. Employers want to ensure you have the endurance to handle the various challenges that will be thrown at you. People often see work as a sprint and grind, working excessive hours leading to burnout and quitting. Yes, you will have to work hard. Sometimes you may have to put in extra hours but then sometimes you may be able to take your foot off the gas. Enjoy those moments.

YOUR BEST 3-5 STORIES

Now, there are a million questions you can potentially prepare for in your interview. It is very easy to get overwhelmed while prepping, and run in a thousand different directions. Instead, think of your best 3-5 stories and mold them to the potential questions. What do I mean by that?

Instead of preparing individual answers for the following questions, have your story be flexible where you can articulate it to each possible version of the questions.

- Tell me a time you had to go above and beyond for a customer?

- Tell me a time you had to be persistent to change someone's mind?

- Tell me about a time you had to think outside the box?

Going above and beyond for the customer usually requires persistence, right? And probably goes a long way to help them change their mind? Not to mention going above and beyond is already outside the box so with one story you can answer 3 different versions of this question. Use that mindset when crafting your stories to help you prepare for the unknown. That way you can take your 3-5 most impactful stories and have them ready rather than 50 memorized different answers.

ADDITIONAL QUESTIONS

1. Tell me about a time you made a mistake and what you did to fix it.

2. When you worked on multiple projects, how did you prioritize?

3. Give an example of how you set goals and achieve them.

4. How do you handle a challenge? Give an example.

5. Tell me about a time when your organizational skills helped you succeed.

6. Provide me with an example of how you handled change in the workplace.

7. What's been the toughest criticism you received so far in your career? What did you do with it?

8. How do you manage change?

Chapter 15

ASKING THE RIGHT QUESTIONS IN THE INTERVIEW

After you cruise through the behavioral interview questions and any other question the recruiter or hiring manager has for you, they will inevitably say, "Do you have any questions for me?"

One of the biggest mistakes inexperienced candidates make is not having any questions to ask. You 100% need to have questions prepared to ask.

Make sure the questions you ask are thoughtful, strategic, and memorable if possible. You want to ask questions that show you have a deep understanding of the opportunity in front of you. Here are ones I have used in the past that have resonated well with people.

ESSENTIAL QUESTIONS

WHAT SEPARATES A GREAT PERFORMER FROM A GOOD PERFORMER IN THIS ROLE?

This shows initiative and that you not only want to succeed but be a top performer. It demonstrates your mentality to be a sponge and learn from other people who have been successful before you.

What do you envision being the biggest challenge for someone stepping into this role?

Sometimes you will get an answer specific to the role, but other times people will provide feedback that is specific to you for this opportunity. Understanding the biggest challenge is key because now you potentially have an opportunity to address it right there and then or in the next interview if you make it to the next round. This will demonstrate to the interviewer that you can think strategically and anticipate upcoming obstacles.

WHAT HAS BEEN YOUR FAVORITE THING ABOUT THE COMPANY CULTURE? AND IF YOU COULD GIVE YOURSELF A PIECE OF ADVICE WHEN YOU FIRST STARTED, WHAT WOULD THAT BE?

This question is significant for two reasons. People want to make sure you fit in the culture, so it's important you are insistent about reiterating to them that you love the culture and would love an opportunity to work there (Note—every company will say they have a great culture, so take what they say with a grain of salt).

But if most of the people during the interview process seem stressed, nervous, or distant, this may be an indicator of poor culture. Sometimes people have off days and that is understandable, but if everyone you connect with during the interview process is not someone you want to work with then it's probably not the right fit.

The second part of the question is important because people like to be asked questions that are different and stick out. Invariably, people love to talk about themselves and many love giving advice. This question allows you to appeal to that desire of the individual while hopefully learning valuable insight about the organization.

WHAT QUESTIONS AM I NOT ASKING THAT I SHOULD BE?

This tends to be my second to last question. I use it to identify any blind spots. Perhaps there was an area that I didn't ask about and could use this as a chance to address it immediately. 90% of the time people appreciated the question, but I did have a poor experience once with an individual who said it was an unfair question and too broad. Just another life lesson; you can't please everyone. So, take that for what it is worth. I am still a fan of it and continue to ask it.

ADDITIONAL QUESTION IDEAS—DEPENDING ON TIME

Where Are You in the Hiring Process?

If the recruiter tells you they are about to extend an offer to another candidate, then that helps you manage your expectations. It doesn't mean it is hopeless as the candidate could turn down the offer or something else can happen. But it is good to be realistic.

What Does a Potential Career Path Look Like?

You always want to be thinking about growth. Some companies have formal professional development programs while others do it more "on the fly." It is good to be grounded to know what potential opportunities exist, and if there is a chance that they align with what you want in the future. Obviously, that is far out in advance, and things can change between now and then, but having a north star is important.

Why Is This Role Open?

This can be a good barometer to learn more about the organization without asking. If the role is open because they promoted someone from within that is a good sign. If it is because the prior person quit, then you know there is a possibility the role has a lot of turnover. It's also possible the role is brand new to the organization. If that is the case, then you will need to understand that it is probably not as defined as other jobs. If you are someone who doesn't like ambiguity, then it might not be a good fit.

Ask a Question About Something They Said Earlier

For example, if while answering a prior question, they brought up how someone has recently excelled in their management training program, and you haven't discussed that yet, then it would be a good time to ask them to expand on the program. This shows you are a good listener, can think in the moment, and didn't just memorize some good questions. It also shows you are interested in professional development.

Company- or Person-Specific Question

Earlier we talked about the importance of doing research ahead of time.

Let's say you are interviewing for a sales position, and the person you are interviewing with was on a sales podcast. Listen to it and ask a strategic question that ties in what they said on the podcast with the role you are interviewing for. For example:

> "For my next question: While I was preparing for this interview, I found a podcast you were on that broke down the most effective sales software tools. Out of all the ones you listed, like Salesforce,

Outreach, and Gong, which ones do you currently have, and which ones are you considering as you grow the sales organization? And why?"

Why is this effective? This will separate you from most of the candidates. This is memorable. Never forget that there are other people who are competing for the role. And being remembered is half the battle with how many candidates these people interview.

Also, this shows you are willing to come to the table prepared. You are showing the interviewer you know how to find unique ways to connect the dots and are a strategic thinker. And it shows you are proactive; they didn't ask you to do this. You did it on your own which is rare for many candidates.

Now, this strategy works even if you can't find anything about your interviewer. Just try to dig deeper on the company for any recent press releases and ask a strategic question around that information.

THE CLOSER QUESTION

"Based on my background, skills, professional experience/education, and our conversation today, do you have any hesitations moving me on to the next round (or offering me the job in the final round)? And if so, could I have a chance to address them?"

Now, this question is phenomenal because it helps close the interview. Most of the time you can tell how you did based on the nonverbals of the person answering.

Sometimes they will say that they need to convene as a group and discuss. That can be code for, "No, we don't want to move you on to the next round" in an attempt to avoid confrontation. Other times it is sincere, and they must discuss as a group and will let you know.

And sometimes the recruiter or hiring manager will come right out and say they like you and you're on to the next round. If this is the case, it can be beneficial to attempt to schedule the next interview before hopping off the call. Once you hop off the call, there is always a chance that the next interview won't get scheduled. Most of the time it will. I have experienced situations where they tell me on the phone that I am on to the next round, and someone will reach out with next steps. Then they make an offer to someone else in the interim, and therefore I am no longer a candidate in the running. That is not common, but I want to make you aware of potential outcomes.

MANAGING THE CLOCK

When interviewing with people, sometimes you will get someone who loves to talk. These people will consume most of the time chatting. Or you will have people who barely speak. Regardless, it is on you to be aware of the time left in the interview.

Sometimes people will leave you 20 minutes in a 30-minute interview to ask questions. Other times they will leave you five minutes. In either case, it is critical that you ask the closing question even if that means forgoing all the other questions you prepared. Why is this one so important?

It lets you know what the interviewer is thinking! Likely, the responses will fall into one of these buckets:

- "I enjoyed our conversation today; I have no hesitations moving you on to the next round. We will be in touch."

- "I enjoyed our conversation today, but will need to circle up with the rest of the team about potential next steps."

- "You know, the only thing that sticks out to me is _____."

A few potential hesitations could include:

- "I appreciate your enthusiasm, but there seems to be a lack of experience."

- "You interview well, but it appears you have had several jobs in a short period of time. That does give me pause."

- "You are clearly bright, but it doesn't seem like your background is aligned with this opportunity."

If you find someone pushing back and letting you know what their hesitation is, then you get an opportunity to address it head on! Do not throw in the towel now. It can be hard to take criticism, or anything perceived as such. Remain calm and do your best to answer to the best of your ability.

Sometimes their concern is something you can clearly address that you didn't get a chance to speak about. Maybe they want to know if you ever prospected (find potential customers in sales) before, and in your prior conversation it never came up. Here is the perfect chance to illustrate that you have prospected, and did it effectively.

Other times you can't change their mind in the end. That is okay, too, as there are plenty of jobs for you in this world and you can use this experience as a learning opportunity.

Chapter 16

THE UNWRITTEN RULES

Interviewing is strange, since there are a bunch of unwritten rules that everyone has agreed to, even if they seem silly.

Never trash your prior employer or boss. Be diplomatic.

I do not care how awful your prior employer or boss was for you. Do not bash them. It will come across as unprofessional, undiplomatic, and lacking self-awareness. Everyone has had bad bosses and experiences. The key is to say that without coming out and saying it.

Instead of saying, "My boss was a tyrant and he kept holding me back," try something like this: "I am extremely thankful for my time at _____, but I outgrew the opportunity, and I am looking to take on more responsibility in my next role."

QUESTIONS TO AVOID ASKING

HOW MANY HOURS DO YOU WORK A DAY/WEEK? WHAT'S THE WORK-LIFE BALANCE?

This makes it seem like you don't want to work hard. To be clear, it is 100% alright, frankly encouraged, to want a job that has a great life work balance.

You need to understand, it is a delicate topic from the employer's perspective. Explore alternative ways to seek that information. Perhaps, wait until you connect with someone who will be a peer and ask them about their typical day/week. If they share how they constantly work late nights and weekends to keep up with the work, then there is your answer.

HOW MUCH WILL I MAKE?

This is the elephant in the room. Everyone wants to know compensation. But when you phrase it as listed above it comes across as presumptuous you get the role, and you are entitled to a certain salary.

Often the recruiter will ask you your desired compensation, as we discussed earlier in Chapter 14, but sometimes they will come out and share it. If the topic doesn't come up and you are nearing the end of the interview, you can politely ask "Can you help me understand a potential compensation range for people in this role?"

ALWAYS DRESS UP

You will never be negatively evaluated in an interview for overdressing unless they specifically told you to wear specific attire that you did not abide by. Getting dressed up shows you take the opportunity seriously, and it is a sign of respect. The worst thing you can do is disqualify yourself for an opportunity by not being dressed professionally.

The definition "professionally dressed" can be flexible, but I would encourage you to stick with the classical suit and tie for men and a blazer, button-up, or cardigan for women.

BE CALM AND CONFIDENT

Employers want someone who is calm and confident. It can be challenging to exude this during a stressful interview, but there are a few things you can do.

- Prepare before the interview. The more prepared you are, the more confident you will feel.

- Interview at several companies so that you don't have all your eggs in one basket.

- Have a cup of coffee before your interview for an extra little pick-me-up.

- Practice perspective taking, and remind yourself that this is just one job interview.

BE AUTHENTIC, BUT DON'T OVERSHARE

Authenticity in corporate America is very different from authenticity with a romantic partner or friends. Employers will say we want you to be your authentic self at work. It sounds great, but it's more lip service than anything. "Authentic" from a corporate perspective means showing enough of your personality while simultaneously avoiding topics that are too personal for work, especially anything relating to the politics, sex, and religion. If you are wondering if something is inappropriate for work, then it probably is and would be in your best interest to just not bring it up.

Also, if you have a side hustle or want to pursue one, it is probably best not to share with your employer. They can view it as a potential distraction to the job.

SOFT SKILLS

Most employers look for people with the right soft skills. Attitude, curiosity, and work ethic are a few examples of soft skills. And those qualities are arguably more important than technical skills early in your career because your employer will teach you what you need to know or will learn through experience on the job. Soft skills are much harder to teach. Be coachable and you will set yourself apart from the competition.

DIPLOMATIC ANSWERS

Below, on the left, are a few examples of how you may feel, but on the right is how you should communicate these feelings in the interview process.

HOW YOU FEEL	DIPLOMATIC ANSWER
My job was so boring.	I am excited to pursue my next chapter with more responsibility.
Management had no idea what they were doing, so I had to do it.	[Insert company] gave me frontline experience on [insert action], because of their unique structure.
All my friends and coworkers left.	We underwent a realignment at the organization where the culture has shifted, and this is part of the reason I am excited to be speaking with you today.
They don't pay me enough.	I am looking for an opportunity to take on additional responsibility and grow professionally.

Chapter 17

WHAT IF I DON'T GET THE JOB?

You just experienced what 99% of the population experiences at some point in life. It sucks. There is no debating that. Especially if you have gone through a bunch of interviews with the company and find out at the end you didn't get it. However, it is important to keep some perspective; you should be proud of yourself for doing your best. Not everything will work out. If you did not perform the way you wanted, take solace knowing that there will be more interviews down the road.

WHAT CAN YOU DO?

While you cannot control the outcome, you can control your actions. Even when getting turned down from an opportunity, you should send an email expressing gratitude for the chance to interview at their company. I do not care if you are sad, pissed, indifferent, etc. Sending a thank you email after a declination is the high road, and your future self will thank you.

In addition, you can use this as an opportunity to get valuable feedback about why you did not get the job, how to improve, and let them know you would be interested if things ever change.

Do not be surprised if some companies won't share much about why it didn't work out. They may state they want to "protect the integrity of the hiring process." That can be a common response, but you won't know without asking.

Here is an example message you can send.

Hi ____,

While that was not the outcome I was striving for, I appreciate you letting me know.

Would you be open to sharing any feedback, so that I can learn from this experience and potentially earn a future opportunity to work at _____?

Best,

_____

WHY DIDN'T IT WORK OUT?

If the company where you interviewed doesn't share why you were turned down, there are several potential reasons you could consider.

POTENTIAL REASONS

- Another candidate had more relevant experience.

- Someone else gelled better with the team and culture.

- The company promoted someone internally.

- Sales are down, and the organization is freezing hiring until next year.

- The company already extended an offer since you are early in the inter-view process.

There could be a myriad of reasons why it didn't work, and you may never know the full truth. But just because this opportunity didn't work out it has no bearing on your worth as an individual. Work is one portion of our life, not our entire identity so do NOT beat yourself up too much.

I have countless friends who have wrapped up their entire identity into their job. And when the job isn't going well, they internalize that as a re-flection of who they are as an individual. We are so much more than just our job, so don't let it control your whole life. This will make it easier to navigate the tough times if your company makes a mistake, because they are prone to that.

A famous mistake made by Facebook is the sto-ry of Brian Acton. Brian was rejected by Face-book for a job in 2009. He later went on to cre-ate WhatsApp and sell it to Facebook for $19 billion dollars. Brian's case is an extreme out-lier but is an example of how companies don't always have it all figured out and can miss out on some of the most talented people.

YOUR IDENTITY

The trap people fall into (including myself):

Reality: Work is just a piece of your identity, not the whole thing.

Chapter 18

EVALUATING FINAL OFFERS

Congratulations! Getting an offer letter feels great, and even better when you have more than one to choose from. That is a good problem to have! If you find yourself in that position, this is the perfect time to re-examine your values to identify which offer lines up best with you. A few things you might want to keep in mind; what is the career trajectory for each opportunity, do you like your hiring manager, and do they seem knowledgeable, do you like your coworkers/peers, and what is the company's projected growth. A company that is growing has tons of opportunities. One that is in decline does not.

Also, just because a company offers you a job, which does not mean you have to accept it. It is important to understand your own value and worth. For example, when I was first out of college, I interviewed at a company I was so excited to work for. I made it through the rigorous interview process and was offered a job for a $25k salary. I was devastated because I knew this was well below market value, and they were not willing to negotiate. I ended up turning it down and a few weeks later had an offer for $58k plus bonuses. But this story brings up another good consideration: How do you negotiate a salary?

HOW TO NEGOTIATE

Negotiating with companies can be hit or miss. Sometimes they will budge, but other times they won't. If you are just starting your career and trying to negotiate with Amazon, that can be difficult because they have a thousand candidates waiting behind you who would like that opportunity. If you are interviewing at a smaller company and you have another offer on the table, you may have a better chance. Generally, when it comes to negotiation, whoever cares less wins.

EXAMPLE SCENARIO

Company 1 - $60k Base Salary (not your first choice)

Company 2 - $50k Base Salary (your ideal company)

If you find yourself in this fortunate position, you can try to negotiate with Company 2. The worst they can do is say no. They most likely will not rescind the offer at this point unless you somehow really offend them.

I have had success framing the discussion like this:

> "Hi Jessica! Thank you again for the offer letter. I am very grateful for the opportunity. I love the culture at _____, and would love to work as a(n) _____ here. However, for full transparency, I do have another offer on the table for $60k. I was hoping you could help get me to that number, or at least closer to it, and

I would be willing to sign the paperwork
tonight."

Now if you pursue this route, you should accept
the offer as you said you were going to. If you
try to negotiate another raise after this, it will
leave a bad taste in their mouth, and they may
move on from you as a candidate.

Let's explore why this is effective. First, you are
telling the recruiter you love the company and
would like to work for the hiring manager, and
it never hurts to slightly "stroke the ego" of your
potential hiring manager (especially when what
you are saying is factual).

Second, when you have another offer on the
table, it makes this conversation more relaxed
because you know even if they say no, you can
walk away and take a higher paying job.

Third, the fact that you tell them you are willing
to sign if they hit that number (or are close)
gives them a target to aim for internally and an
incentive to get you onboarded.

Chances are, if they decided to offer you anything, it will be a modest increase, but something is better than nothing. And as you begin

to build your skillset and become more valuable in the marketplace, you will be able to negotiate better and better compensation packages.

COMPENSATION PACKAGES

So what really goes into compensation packages? Think of this as everything you get for working there. Most people have heard of salary, bonuses, 401k, and health insurance, but there is so much more.

SALARY

This is what you get every two weeks or on a periodic schedule. When people say they make $50,000 or $150,000 a year, this is what they are commonly referencing.

BONUSES

Many companies offer annual, semiannual, or quarterly bonuses. Some are a flat amount, such as a $5,000 bonus for reaching a quantified goal in a specific amount of time.

Others are tied to a percentage of your salary. For example, let's say you make $100,000, and the company says, you can earn an annual bonus up to 15% of your salary, which would be 15,000. Most of the time, this is tied to your individual performance and company performance. Some companies will say if the company misses its goal, no bonuses are paid out. Others are paid out as a portion if the goal is partially hit. However, if the company exceeds their goals, then your actual bonus may surpass that 15%. Always review the fine print when reviewing your compensation structure.

Also, some companies will offer a sign on bonus. This is an extra incentive to attract talent and often comes with an agreement to stay with the company for a minimum amount of time.

EMPLOYEE STOCK PURCHASE PLANS (ESPPS)

ESPPs are for publicly traded companies and can be a great opportunity for you to enhance your total earnings. The ESPP allows you to buy your company stock at a discount, often ranging from a 5%–15% discount of current market value (current price per share).

The company will have an "open enrollment period" for a couple weeks where you get to decide if you want to contribute anywhere from 0–10% (10% is usually the max) of total earnings (salary and bonuses) toward the program.

After the "open enrollment period" ends "the offering period" starts. This is where every two weeks (or pay period) the company will take money out of your paycheck to set aside to purchase the stock at the discount on a specified purchase date in the future.

Most programs will either have two different "offering periods" lasting 6 months each, or 4 offering periods for three months a piece.

For easy math, let's say you make $120,000 a year and the company offers a 15% discount for their ESPP program that has two offering periods a year. You decide to contribute 10% of your earnings to the ESPP.

- Annual Salary: $120,000

- Monthly Paycheck: $10,000

- Contribution Amount: 10% of Paycheck

- ESPP Total per Paycheck: $1,000 ($10,000 paycheck * 10% contribution amount)

- ESPP Total at End of Offering Period: $6,000 ($1,000 per paycheck * 6 month offering period)

Now your employer is going to take that $6,000 and purchase company stock for you. Let's pretend that the stock is $100 a share. Don't forget that you get a 15% discount, so you will get to acquire the stock at $85 instead of $100:

- Market: $100 per share * 60 total shares = $6,000 total

- Your rate: $85 per share * 70.588 shares = $6,000 total

Essentially, you were able to buy 10 more shares than other people with the same $6,000 because of that discount. Meaning the true value, you own is $7,058.8 ($100 per share * 70.588 shares) Now you can either sell these shares immediately to make a 15% return on your money or hold on to the stock in hopes it continues to rise.

Let's add one more benefit that is sometimes included in these programs and it is called a "look back period." We talked about how there are two offering periods. Well, a look back period allows you to purchase stock at whichever price point is lower at the end of the offering period.

Continuing the analogy above, let's say you have two offering periods:

- Offering Period 1: Nov – May and the stock was $50

- Offering Period 2: May – Nov and the stock was $100

Even though the stock price is $100 at the end of the second offering period in May you get to purchase the stock for 15% of the lower of two prices, which is $50 per share.

- Market: $100 per share * 60 total shares = $6,000 total

- Your rate: $42.5 per share * 141.17 shares = $6,000 total investment

That $6,000 you invested is now worth $14,117 ($100 per share * 141.17 shares).

If you believe in the company's long-term future the ESPP can be a lucrative perk. However, understand nothing is guaranteed in the stock market. Everything could drop tomorrow, a week from now, 5 years in the future, or 100 years. No one truly knows.

RESTRICTED STOCK UNITS (RSUS)

Restricted stock units (RSU) are another way for employers to compensate you with stock. These units of stock are often gifted to you over periods of time. This is different from the ESPP where you must purchase the stock.

For example, employers may grant you $30,000 worth of RSUs with a 4-year vesting schedule. A 4-year vesting schedule means each year, you will obtain 25% of the $30,000 (aka $7,500). But the IRS views that $7,500 as income from a tax perspective when you obtain the RSUs so be sure to work with your tax professional.

Often, companies will grant a fixed amount. This example was $30,000, but the stock could be worth more, less, or the same by the time you officially obtain your grant.

RSUs are often a part of what is called a long-term incentive plan (LTIP). The company is trying to align incentives to ensure you don't leave the company after a year or two.

401K

A 401k is a retirement vehicle that allows you to contribute up to $19,500 a year tax free to save and invest for retirement. You can put this money in investments and let it grow tax free and withdraw the money without penalty at 65. Great compensation plans will offer a 401k with a company match. A company match means for every dollar you contribute to your 401k retirement the company will match your dollar for dollar. Oftentimes the company match has a maximum limit at a specific percentage (example up to 3% of salary) of your contributions or a flat cap of roughly $3,000 max.

HEALTH INSURANCE

Health insurance is top of mind for most people. In my opinion, if you don't work in insurance, health insurance can be very confusing. Heck, I could write a whole book on this topic because there is so much. But I will keep to the CliffsNotes.

There are several types of plans that each have their own pros and cons:

- High Deductible Health Plan (HDHP)

- Health Maintenance Organization (HMO)

- Point of Service (POS)

- Exclusive Provider Organization (EPO)

- Preferred Provider Organization (PPO)

A quality health insurance plan provided by your employer will have a reasonable monthly premium (amount you have to pay each month) and accessibility to quality care. Now, "reasonable" and "quality" can be rather subjective. Perhaps the employer will disclose upfront that they pay for 80% of your premium, or they haven't raised premiums for several years; these can be two indicators of an organization that is focused on providing for their employees. If you have questions about the health insurance, do not hesitate to ask the recruiter and they will most likely be able to answer them or put you in contact with a human resources (HR) contact in the organization to inform you.

HEALTH SAVINGS ACCOUNT (HSA)

Per Healthcare.gov: "A type of savings account that lets you set aside money on a pre-tax basis to pay for qualified medical expenses. By using untaxed dollars in a Health Savings Account (HSA) to pay for deductibles, copayments, coinsurance, and some other expenses, you may be able to lower your overall health care costs."

HSAs are only available for high deductible health plans (HDHP). The current maximum contribution for an HSA is $3,600 for an individual and $7,200 for a family (check with the IRS if these numbers have changed). Great employers will match your contributions to your HSA up to a specific dollar amount, similar to the 401k example we discussed earlier.

FLEXIBLE SPENDING ACCOUNT (FSA)

Per Healthcare.gov: "An arrangement through your employer that lets you pay for many out-of-pocket medical expenses with tax-free dollars. Allowed expenses include insurance copayments and deductibles, qualified prescription drugs, insulin, and medical devices." The intent of the FSA is to spend all the money before the end of the year. According to Healthcare.Gov, "If money is left at the end of the year, the employer can offer one of two options (not both):

- You get 2.5 more months to spend the left-over money.

- You can carry over up to $500 to spend the next plan year."

ADDITIONAL BENEFITS

Paid Time Off (PTO)

This is how many days of vacation/sick time you get each year. Every employer is different; some will even offer unlimited PTO. Double-check the fine print in the policy to ensure it aligns with what you want.

Pet Insurance

Some employers will offer to cover partial premiums to help provide pet insurance for our furry friends.

Sabbatical

A sabbatical is a paid leave of absence after working a specified number of years. It is not very common with employers, but with ones I have seen, they usually work for five years and get a one month paid sabbatical.

Tuition Reimbursement

Most companies will offer some type of tuition reimbursement up to a certain dollar amount. Some tuition reimbursement programs will require you to earn a certain grade to qualify for reimbursement. Example: If you get all C's, they may only reimburse you for half of the tuition. Many of these programs will require you to stay with the employer for a year or two, or you will have to pay back the employer the tuition they reimbursed you for.

Paid Paternal Leave

Companies continue to invest in their paid paternal leave policy to attract and retain talent.

This is the paid time off after you have a baby. A decent maternity (mother) leave policy is 12 weeks and paternity (father) leave is 6 weeks. Some of the most forward-thinking companies offer much more generous time off such as up to 6 months or a year. While other companies have not come around to updating their paid paternal leave policy and have limited leave.

Various Perks

A newer trend is companies may offer subscriptions to various software. A few examples: HingeHealth (virtual physical therapy), Teladoc (virtual doctor), and Wondr (weight loss software). The perks and benefits for employees continue to evolve, so keep an eye out for the latest trends.

SALES COMPENSATION

Sales is different from almost any other role in that typically the harder you work, the more you make. In most other roles, you must wait for a raise, promotion, or bonus, but sales are structured differently.

SALES COMMISSION

Sales Commission is when you get a percentage of each sale paid out to you in cash. For easy math, let's say you sell software that the customer buys for $1,000 and your commission percentage is 10%. For every sale of $1,000, you get $100.

Most of the time, salespeople have a quota, a minimum number of sales you need to achieve.

Pretend your annual quota is $200,000. With a 10% commission rate that puts you at $20,000 in addition to your base salary. If you don't reach your quota, you don't make that commission.

SALES ACCELERATORS/KICKERS

The best companies offer salespeople not only commission at a generous rate, but they will also pay above that rate once you achieve quota. Revisiting our prior example, let's say you get 10% commission on any deal. After you hit 100% of your quota, anything after that they may pay you at 15%, 17.5%, 20% or whatever it is the company decides. You could potentially be making more on the same deal than if it were closed prior to obtaining quota.

Why do companies do this? Well, they want to make sure salespeople continue to perform. They don't want someone to hit quota in the first quarter and take the rest of the year off. This keeps people incentivized.

SALES AWARD TRIPS

Some companies will offer special trips for top performers, this is often called presidents club. Typically, these trips are all expenses paid to somewhere fun and beautiful. It could be in a desirable location in the US, island resorts, Europe, etc. The best award trips allow you to have one guest of your choice, with all expenses paid, to accompany you on the trip.

SALES PRODUCT SPECIFIC INCENTIVES

Let's say the company you work for has twenty products, and they just released a brand-new product that management wants you to push. They might increase your commission rate on that specific product/solution to increase adoption out on the market. For example, instead of paying out 10% for regular products, the brand-new product pays out a 25% commission.

SALES PERFORMANCE INCENTIVE FUND: SPIF

SPIFs are used to reward salespeople for a specific objective. Perhaps they will give a bonus to the sales rep who makes the most calls, sets the most appointments, has the best close rate, etc. It is up to sales leadership to decide on a specific objective/metric they want the team to achieve. Generally, SPIFs are shorter term in nature, like a fiscal quarter (3 months) or two. They are often rolled out in the form of a contest but not always. Really depends on the unique needs of that specific organization.

TRAVELING ROLES

There are some jobs that require you to travel all the time, especially consultants. If you are thinking about a life on the road, there are a few things to consider.

CREDIT CARDS

Are you allowed to put the charges on your cards and get reimbursed? Do you have to use the company card? If you can use your own credit cards and you are diligent about your finances, you can reap tons of rewards and promotions. Let's say you open a new Hilton card and spend $3,000 in the first 3 months. You will earn 100,000 bonus points. These points can be used to redeem free complimentary nights at Hilton hotels. If the company allows you to use your credit card to pay for these expenses and get reimbursed, then you get to take advantage of these special promotions. Not to mention it will most likely help you obtain a higher status in their rewards program that comes with additional perks.

PER DIEM POLICY

Per diems is the money you get paid for meals while traveling for work. Companies usually have set rates but may vary based on city. This is advantageous to you because typically it is somewhere around:

- $18 for breakfast

- $20 for lunch

- $36 for dinner

That's a total of $74 a day. Let's say you travel 4 days a week, so you get $296 a week. If you travel 45 weeks out of the year, that is $13,320 tax free. Granted you will probably want to use some of that to go out to eat. But if you are thrifty, by eating less expensive meals or buying groceries in your new work city, you can pocket a significant amount of that money. Consider it a $13,000 raise for yourself.

COMPENSATION PACKAGES

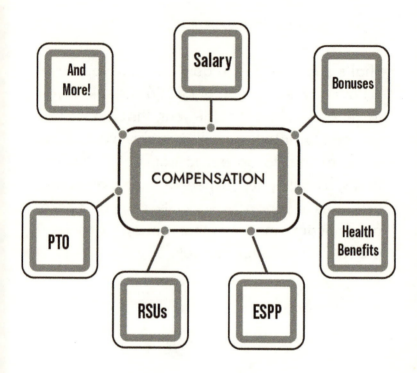

Chapter 19

HIT THE GROUND RUNNING

Alright, this is where the rubber hits the road. You accepted your first job, and you want to make a great first impression.

Here are a few things you can do to set yourself up for success.

KEY TIPS

- Always show up early (in person or online) or on time.

- Take notes and send out after meetings without being asked (unless sensitive information).

- If you set a meeting, create an agenda and put it in the calendar invite.

- Try not to ask the same question twice.

- Understand you can always control your attitude and effort.

- Be a sponge and learn everything you can.

- Be curious and ask why.

- Be proactive.

- Have a clear understanding of expectations from your manager.

- Pick up a few business books.

- Be a continuous learner.

- If you don't know what someone is saying to you in an email, pick up the phone and call them.

- Enjoy yourself. Life is short. Don't sweat the small stuff.

Chapter 20

MADE A MISTAKE?

Sometimes in life you can do everything right and things still don't work out. Don't beat yourself up if you find yourself in a position you don't like. Maybe you don't like the culture, or perhaps your boss is the worst. It can be easy to have thoughts like, *I can't believe I am so stupid for taking this job*, or, *I better wait a couple years before looking, so I don't look like a job hopper*.

Now, I am not saying just because you feel bad means you are blameless. You need to take stock of the situation and try to be as objective as you can about it. Ask yourself questions like the ones below:

- Did I give it enough time?

- Can it get better?

- Why am I feeling this way?

- Am I getting enough sleep?

- Am I eating right?

- Am I exercising?

- Am I the only one feeling this way?

- How can I improve?

- How can I reframe?

And if after all that, you still decide it is best for you to move on, then I recommend giving yourself slack. I found myself in this position before and I was being rather hard on myself about the situation. When confiding in a mentor, he asked me "How much time did you spend with your boss before getting hired? 45 minutes? If you could have predicted how he would have reacted on a random Tuesday when things are not going well then you and I should be playing the lottery because you'd have to be the luckiest person to be 100% right."

This doesn't mean the process you went through is broken. Rather, you learned something new, and you know now what you don't want. Like a true professional, you can use this to learn and grow.

Don't give up, don't ever give up. The right opportunity for you is out there. Maybe it's taking longer than you would like, but that's life. There is an old expression that "we make plans, and God laughs."

Keep your head up and keep moving.

REVIEWS

As you may know, many of us authors are at the mercy of our readers. And it can be a scary thing releasing a book you have been working on for years out into the wild.

With that being said, I hope you got some value out of it—at least learned something new. And if that is the case, would you be open to leaving an Amazon review? Reviews greatly improve chances of showing up in rankings when people are searching. You have absolutely no obligation to leave a review. But if you do, I will be eternally grateful.

ABOUT THE AUTHOR

Tim Luchtefeld grew up in a small town called Morton, Illinois. He attended the University of Northern Iowa, where he double majored in Management Information Systems and Marketing.

After graduation he started working for a leading healthcare technology company leading complex projects and selling enterprise software, robotics, and capital equipment to hospitals.

He went back to school to earn his MBA through the University of Illinois, and shortly after obtained his Project Management Professional (PMP) certification.

He currently works at a technology company and is passionate about helping others grow their career.

Tim Luchtefeld, MBA, PMP

REFERENCES

Arruda, W. (2016, September 6). *The Most Damaging Myth About Branding*. Forbes. https://www.forbes.com/sites/williamarru da/2016/09/06/the-most-damaging-myth- about-branding/?sh=3df05b825c4f

Flexible Spending Account (FSA). (n.d.). Healthcare.gov. https://www.healthcare.gov/ glossary/flexible-spending-account-fsa/

Health Savings Account (HSA). (n.d.). Healthcare. gov. https://www.healthcare.gov/glossary/ health-savings-account-hsa/

Popomaronis, T. (2019 April 17). *Here's how many Google job interviews it takes to hire a Googler*. CNBC. https://www.cnbc.com/

2019/04/17/heres-how-many-google-job-interviews-it-takes-to-hire-a-googler.html

Resume Example. (n.d.). Chicago Booth. https://www.chicagobooth.edu/-/media/secure/alumni/career-services/resume-template-more-than-10-years-alumni.docx?la=en&hash=A409D506635BA813E475E48E0AA4417CE89D79AD

Sherman, E. (2019, March 14). *WhatsApp Co-Founder Brian Acton Repeats Call to Delete Facebook.* Fortune. https://fortune.com/2019/03/14/whatsapp-facebook/

Town, P. (2018, January 4). *The Important Differences Between Price And Value.* Forbes. https://www.forbes.com/sites/forbesfinancecouncil/2018/01/04/the-important-differences-between-price-and-value/?sh=361dec244237

Wei, W. (2010, October 5). *Ideas Are A Dime A Dozen, Execution Is All That Matters.* Insider. https://www.businessinsider.com/ideas-are-a-dime-a-dozen-execution-is-all-that-matters-2010-10